POETIC INSPIRATION

"A dictation from a higher place"

Leading Edge Poetry in Alignment
with Abraham's Teachings of the
Law of Attraction

MICHAEL OELE

Rushmore Press LLC
www.rushmorepress.com
1 888 733 9607

Copyright © 2019 by Michael Oele.

ISBN   Softcover   978-1-950818-16-7

All rights reserved. No part of this publication may be reproduced, distributed, or transmitted in any form or by any means, including photocopying, recording, or other electronic or mechanical methods, without the prior written permission of the publisher, except in the case of brief quotations embodied in critical reviews and certain other non-commercial uses permitted by copyright law.

Printed in the United States of America.

TABLE OF CONTENTS

Abundant 1
Alignment 3
Allowing 5
Appreciation 7
Attraction 9
Beautiful 11
Contrast 13
Creator 15
Enlightened 17
Focus 19
Freedom 21
I am 23
Imagination 25
Manifestation 27
One 29
Peace 31
Prosperous 33
Reflection 35
Thank you 37
For Now 39

DEDICATION

I am honored and certain of my desire to dedicate this book, Poetic Inspiration, to Esther Hicks, Jerry, (her beloved) and Abraham, the collective consciousness Esther brings forth by quieting her mind through her practice of meditation.

It was obvious to me, that while I know that we are all in this together, the work Esther shares with all whom are ready to experience a broader perspective, became pivotal for this book to come to manifestation.

Esther's commitment to her work has evoked an expansion, that equals the asking of many, me included, who seek personal and global advancement.

The leading edge stimulating thoughts that come forth from our asking, are answered and stand true in alignment to the principal of everlasting life.

Thank you eternally Esther Hicks.

In appreciation and love,

Michael Oele.

FOREWORD

Michael Oele's book of poetry and images are an inspiration,
and support the presence of alignment for all who read them.
Michaels book is truly a tribute of love for the work of Abraham,
Esther and Jerry Hicks.
A stunningly beautiful book of poetry

Kathleen Arnason
president of Seena publications

PREFACE

It is my privileged desire that wherever you may be in relationship to everything else that is going on in your life, that you allow me to welcome you to explore, in a sense of freedom, to see beauty, and further acknowledge from your unique and important perspective, your inner knowing of well-being.

I simply love you.
Michael Oele

ABUNDANT

I am abundant by nature,
I am abundant in truth,
I am abundant, and have been,
Well before my youth.

I came here knowing of blessings,
And the kingdom of all that is,
I'm consciously aware of my abundant presence,
And that everything already exists.

ALIGNMENT

I love alignment
It's the only assignment

I love you Special
I trust that you will

Knowing of ease
Ease of knowing

Body and mind relaxed
Feeling the flow

Focus is worthy
Fun is fun

Letting it be
Unconditionally

ALLOWING

I am a being, remembering, who I really am,
I come from absolute certainty, a deliberate, expansive plan.

I am joyously empowered, positively pure,
All in one, one in all, cooperative, and sure.

In self-love and appreciation, I take action, I come alive,
Working up the emotional scale,
In frequencies where I can thrive.

My focused thoughts bring feelings, to all the things I do,
Aligning with source energy, magnificent and true.

My passionate dreams and desires, I've come to believe and know,
Honoring the creative process, letting it all flow.

Things are working well for me, I trust, and I allow,
I ask, and it is given, it comes to me somehow.

I know of my worth, I have chosen my birth, from eternal royalty,
I deserve all things, in this life, I'm source and source is me.

APPRECIATION

Temporarily in the gift of the expanding contrast
Turning my cheek ever so slightly
In this moment I am satisfied
I am filled with mindful optimism

Life then reveals the perfection of its truth
I live in a friendly universe
Therefore I am summoned by life to choose appreciation.

Oh, and as I do, kindness speaks
Happiness peaks
The world becomes what it always has been
Expanding joy
Liquid love solidifying in delightful form

ATTRACTION

Writing my life story cover to cover,
I am love, being loved, a full time lover.

Living the richness of my self-pleasing thought,
satisfied in the presence of what I've got.

Treasuring what contrast has naturally stimulated,
anticipating the blessing vibrationally created.

I am a confident believer of eternal youth,
becoming the feeling of my own deepest truth.

Certainty of knowing my decided course,
joyously reaching alignment with Source.

Empowered with blossoming creativity,
abundant in health in happiness and prosperity.

Pure positive emotion with inspired action,
expectant in focused imagined satisfaction.

Unconditionally offering energy of desire,
allowing appreciation to manifest what I admire.

Expanding the perfection of all that is here now,
Graciously accepting and never asking how.

Eagerness for thriving in well-being full of passion,
Co-creating harmony in a universe of attraction.

BEAUTIFUL

Every day is beautiful
Beauty, it may be found
It's in taste, touch, scent, sight and sound.

My life is beautiful
It is mine to behold
In appreciation, I see beauty, simply unfold.

My thoughts are beautiful
They are one of a kind
I think of beauty, in spirit, in body, and open mind.

My feelings are beautiful
I feel so alive
The feeling is freedom, I feel empowered to thrive.

Everything is beautiful,
the perfection I see.
Beauty is everywhere, it's all around me.

Fun is beautiful
It is natural and free
It is fun that creates eternity, beautifully.

I am beautiful
I am just like you, of course
I believe we are in likeness, of our loving source.

Most beautiful

CONTRAST

What is contrast?

Some say enemy
Others say friend
Without opposites
Life would end.

It's all relative
Thoughts brings its kind
It's a perspective
It's a state of mind.

Life's method for expansion
Brings forth a desire
Focus in passion
New things to admire.

Because of its presence
We ask for change
Prefer something different
Or rearrange.

There's no other way
to become the more
Because of contrast
there's much more in store.

Its perfection is obvious
Doesn't always feel that way
we can be oblivious
But it is here to stay.

CREATOR

Thank you source for using me to express and expand.
I know the riches of all that is are presently at hand.

I create my thoughts and my feelings too,
being my truth and aligning with you.

Becoming the more I said I can,
Molding energy of love all at my command.

ENLIGHTENED

Having or showing a rational, modern, well informed outlook.

There is realization

Awareness of genius and brilliance of our inner being
Accepting the empowerment of alignment in joyful remembering

Rejoicing the knowing of the vibrational reality of creation
There lies the consciousness of self actualization

A stream of well-being is the environment of the soul
Appreciation primes the ever increasing flow

Thoughts blended with passion become things
Universal law of attraction mimics and brings

It's an art
The art of allowing

FOCUS

The center of interest

                Thinking
       masterfully   thoughts
         Thy-self   deliberately
      Honoring   Wanting
      willingly   something
    attention   focus   decidedly
      Paying   is the   Feeling
   beautifully   joy of   good
        things   love   purposely
     Imagining   Molding
    intentionally   energy
         desires   creatively
             Loving

FREEDOM

Coming forth and being me,
I knew of freedom and feeling free.

Thinking thoughts in harmony,
of pleasure and ease with liberty.

Exhilarating decision to play and explore,
in joyous expansion and allowing more.

Experiencing jubilation in choices desired,
unique preferences becoming inspired.

The confidence of knowing I am assured,
my thoughts and feelings accurately mirrored.

Aligned with source I live in well being,
what I believe reflects what I am seeing.

Living such freedom bondage may seem real,
the emotional guidance system indicates the feel.

With contrast that is here deliberately for me,
in wisdom I remain stable and free.

Freedom is love passionately expressed,
empowered in good feeling I often possess.

What a beautiful world here for me,
what a glorious time to be free.

I love my given freedom.

I AM

I
am
Joy   W   E
Love   E   X
Hope   L   P
Belief   L   A
Passion   B   N
Freedom   E   D
Optimism | |
Knowledge   N   N
Expectation   G   G
Appreciation
Contentment
Empowerment

IMAGINATION

A true sign of intelligence is the usage of imagination.
Albert Einstein

The imagined life
expediting the dream
knowing in good faith
the vibrational well-being stream

Going with the flow
fondness for inspiration
with awakened consciousness
providing thought creation

Knowing what is wanted
eager with anticipation
feeling good in desire
transformed by imagination

The power of the vision
the motion picture of the mind
as a consequence of Law
the Universe reveals like kind.

MANIFESTATION

I love being in the fields, and in the orchard.

The welcomed warmth of the new season.
The succulent scent rich with sweet pleasing.

Flexible while selecting, in delicious delight.
Looking in awe, far reaching in sight,
of thoughts planted in love, just right.

The harvest of focus, aligned in passion.
The taste of ripe fruit, absolute satisfaction.

Mmmmm manifestation!

ONE

I speak of ease, peace, and harmony,
And the essence of all, that is love to me,

I smile, I hug, I laugh, and I joke,
I converse, I listen, and I care to evoke,

the closeness with you, because it is true,
the love within me, is the love within you.

I believe, I know, I come to expect,
the movement in me, I truly respect,

is natural, and real, as I reach to align,
the kingdom, divine, is yours, and is mine.

In freedom, well-being, appreciation, and passion,
joyously creating, with humor and fun,

Inspired, and feeling the enthusiasm,
I realize, in love, we become one.

PEACE

Paddling the shores of knowing

A gaze into the eyes of love

Greeting the friendship of clarity

Embraced with joyful abundance

Attentive to the sound of ease

Hearing the diversity of freedom

Marveling in the streets of interest

A sleep in a bed of trust

Held by the hands of alignment

A walk in the forest of understanding

Playful on the field of acceptance

Present to the gift of allowing

Resting in the pleasure of passion

Feeling the warmth of eternity

PROSPEROUS

In wisdom

I am prosperous
I am prosperous
$$$$$
$$$$$
$$$$$
$$$$$
$$$$$
I am prosperous
I am prosperous

$$$$$$$
$$$$$$$$
$$$$ $$$$
$$$$ $$$$
$$$$$$$$$$$$
I am prosperous
$$$$ $$$$
$$$$ $$$$
$$$$ $$$$

$$$$$$ $$$$$$
$$$$$$$ $$$$$$$
I am pro   spe rous
I am pro   spe rous
I am   prospe   rous
$$$$ $$$$$ $$$$
$$$$ $$$$ $$$$
$$$$ $$$ $$$$
$$$$ $$ $$$$

REFLECTION

You reflect love

Thank you
hank you
ank you
nk you
k you
you
ou
u
uuuuuuuuuuuuuuuuuuuuuuuuuuuuuuuuuuuu
u
ou
you
k you
nk you
ank you
hank you
Thank you

You reflect love

REFLECTION

THANK YOU

Because I know what I know
And it feels like belief
What I want to shout out is THANK YOU!

At times when I desire a little relief
It is a good time for me to say thank you.

In the process of attracting more in my life
I feel the magnificent words thank you.

In the knowledge of being blessed - begets the best
What a wonderful time to say thank you

As for honoring and appreciating all the rest
It feels natural and good to say thank you.

To have be and do
To love me and you
Perhaps perfect words are thank you

Sincerely
Thank you
Thank you
Thank you.....

FOR NOW

Honor the self,
                (respect, great esteem)

    simply,
                (straightforwardly)

    being,
                (existence)

    honorable.
                (bringing or worthy of honor)

In love and appreciation,
Michael Oele.

www.ingramcontent.com/pod-product-compliance
Lightning Source LLC
Chambersburg PA
CBHW041314110526
44591CB00022B/2915